Contents

The Occupation of Europe   4

The Nazis take over   6

The Nazis and the Holocaust   8

Life for children   16

Life for women   24

Working life   26

Leisure time   28

Undermining religion, creating suspicion   30

Life in the ghettos   32

The Lodz ghetto   36

Special cases   40

A closer look: Living in hiding   44

Timeline   50

Glossary   52

Further reading   54

Places of interest and websites   55

Index   56

Words appearing in the text in bold, **like this**, are explained in the Glossary.

The Occupation of Europe

In 1933 the **Nazi** Party, led by Adolf Hitler, came to power and became the most powerful political party in Germany. The Nazis wanted to create a huge German empire, the **Third Reich**. Between 1938 and 1945, the German army marched into and occupied much of Europe, including Poland, France, the Netherlands and parts of the Soviet Union, nearly defeating the forces of the British Empire, France and the USSR. During this period, the Nazis systematically killed off many people they thought of as '**undesirable**'. The largest group were the **Jewish** people. The Nazis killed between five and six million Jews in what has become known as the **Holocaust**, in an attempt to destroy all the Jewish people in the areas they controlled.

Why did the German army invade?

Once in power, the Nazis banned all other political parties and began trying to create the perfect Nazi state. One thing the Nazis wanted was ***Lebensraum*** – more land for Germans to live in. To begin with, the Nazis took land that had once been part of Germany. But once the German army was on the march it carried on, north, south, east and west of Germany. One of Hitler's beliefs was that a strong country had the right to take over a weaker one.

The German army

When Germany lost the First World War in 1918, the Treaty of Versailles took a lot of land from Germany and reduced the size of its army and navy. When the Nazis took over in 1933, Hitler began to build the army up again, breaking the Treaty of Versailles. The photo shows the German army marching into the Rhineland in 1936. The terms of the Treaty banned the army from this part of Germany, which shared a border with France. Hitler admitted to his generals: 'The 45 hours after the march into the Rhineland were the most nerve-wracking of my life.' His army was still small and he feared that the other European countries would stop it. If they had known what Hitler planned, they might have done so. However, at this point, they were still trying to prevent war.

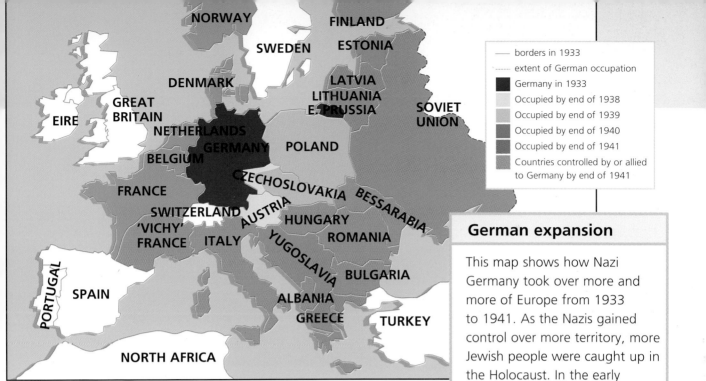

borders in 1933

extent of German occupation

Germany in 1933

Occupied by end of 1938

Occupied by end of 1939

Occupied by end of 1940

Occupied by end of 1941

Countries controlled by or allied to Germany by end of 1941

German expansion

This map shows how Nazi Germany took over more and more of Europe from 1933 to 1941. As the Nazis gained control over more territory, more Jewish people were caught up in the Holocaust. In the early 1930s, many Jews left Germany for the safety of France, the Netherlands or Belgium, only to find these countries taken over by Germany during the war.

Why did no one stop the Nazis?

Other European countries did not try to stop the Nazis for several reasons. One reason was that they did not want another war like the **First World War**. Another was that Hitler did not say: 'I want to take over as much of Europe as possible.' Instead, he claimed he was putting right the injustice of the **Treaty of Versailles**. Many Europeans agreed that the treaty had been too harsh. Hitler began by moving his army into the Rhineland. Then, in 1938, he took over Austria, where over 80 per cent of the population was German. The other major European powers, France, Italy and Britain, then agreed Hitler could make one 'last territorial claim in Europe' and take over the **Sudetenland**, a part of Czechoslovakia. However, in March 1939, he took over the rest of Czechoslovakia and in September 1939, he invaded Poland. At this point, Britain and France, who had promised to help Poland if it was invaded, declared war. They were too late.

While they had been concentrating on peace, Hitler had been preparing for war. In a speech made in 1940, Joseph Goebbels, Hitler's **propaganda** minister, announced: 'When the war is over we want to be masters of Europe.' This book shows what it was like to live in Nazi-occupied Europe.

How do we know?

We know about life in Nazi-occupied Europe from many different sources. People made written accounts, diaries, poems and pictures. We also still have a lot of Nazi propaganda that shows how the Nazis took control of all aspects of life. Lastly, many programmes have been made about the war, which include interviews with all kinds of people who lived in Hitler's Europe.

The Nazis take over

Before the **Nazis** came to power in 1933, Germany was a **democracy**, like most of the rest of Europe. It was also suffering an economic depression. This meant a time of high unemployment, low wages and high prices. The German government had not been able to solve the country's problems. The Nazis claimed democracy wasn't working and promised to make Germany great again. They said Germany needed one political party and one leader – and that was Adolf Hitler.

Enough voters in Germany agreed with the Nazis that they were able to get the most seats in the Reichstag, the German parliament. Once they controlled the Reichstag, the Nazis took over completely by banning all other political parties. They began to turn Germany into the 'perfect' Nazi state. The Nazis' next priority was to expand their *Lebensraum*, which meant finding more 'living-space' for the German people. Their solution was to invade and take over other countries.

Blitzkrieg

Instead of sending in long lines of slow marching soldiers, the Nazis used a new tactic called **blitzkrieg**, or 'lightning war'. First, they sent their planes to bomb the enemy's air force, roads, railways and telephone lines. Then they sent in fast-moving troops. Blitzkrieg was led by tanks, the panzer division and light artillery. These troops were protected by the German air force, which also bombed enemy troops. Most other European armies could not cope with the speed and ferocity of the German advance, and were defeated in a matter of weeks.

'Undesirables'

To the Nazis, all countries, even Germany, had people in it that were '**undesirable**'. People were undesirable because of their **race**, religion, opposition to the Nazis or even their health. **Jewish** people, **Gypsies**, homosexuals, the physically and mentally disabled and **Jehovah's Witnesses** were all considered to be undesirable. Undesirables had to change their ways to fit the Nazi pattern or leave Nazi-occupied lands. If they did neither, then they had to be cut off from 'ordinary **citizens**', even killed. The Gypsies in this photo are being rounded up and taken to **concentration camps**.

Influence

The Germans controlled some countries by influence. This meant that if another country agreed with Nazi views, they were seen as allies and allowed to keep their own government. At the start of the war, Italy, which was ruled by the fascist dictator Mussolini, was one such country. The Nazis also made agreements with the leaders of countries that were not sympathetic to Nazi views. The leaders could still run the country – as long as they ran it the way the Nazis told them to. However, if an allied country did not completely support Nazi policies, it soon became an enemy of Germany instead – this happened to both Italy and the Soviet Union. The German army marched in and influence quickly became occupation.

A different view

The Nazis had strong ideas about **racial superiority**. They treated the people in the countries they took over in different ways, depending on how they fitted into Nazi ideas about race. German soldiers were taught that people such as the Slavs, who included the Poles and the Russians, were 'inferior' races. One soldier advancing into Poland said:

> 'I do not understand how these people are biologically capable of staying alive. Also they live in indescribably filthy conditions. The Polish Jews have alien-looking faces.'

On the other hand, German soldiers were taught that '**Aryans**' were the best race. Although the people of Scandinavia, Britain and France were not as important as the Germans, they were not thought to be *untermenschen*, or 'subhuman', like the Slavs. So the German army, Nazi officials and police behaved far better towards the people of France than they did to the people of Poland – as long as they did as they were told.

The Nazis and the Holocaust

Of all the groups of people that Adolf Hitler despised as 'inferiors', he hated **Jewish** people most. This was clear even before the **Nazis** came to power in Germany. Once they were in power, they began to act against Jews immediately.

Step by step

The Nazis began by passing laws that stopped Jews from working in certain jobs. They moved on to pass laws that stopped Jews using the same transport, schools, public facilities, even park benches as non-Jews. Then they began working to make Germany and the countries it controlled **Judenfrei** – Jew free. In Eastern Europe, Jews were herded into walled-off **ghettos** in cities and were not allowed to live anywhere else. Once Jews were cut off from other people it was easier for the Nazis to go even further against them.

The Holocaust

The Nazis had tried to force Jews in Germany to leave the country before the war. After war broke out, German policy against the Jews became more and more severe. Eventually, they moved on to what they called the 'Final Solution'. This meant setting up 'death camps' at Chelmno, Belzec, Sobibor, Treblinka, Majdanek and Auschwitz-Birkenau to do nothing but kill Jewish people.

Mein Kampf

In 1923, Hitler and the Nazis had tried to take power in Germany by force. They failed and Hitler was sent to prison. While he was in prison the Nazi Party fell apart. Hitler spent eight months in prison and during this time he wrote a book called *Mein Kampf* (which translates as 'My Struggle'), outlining his beliefs. Once the Nazis came to power everyone was expected to read this book. In it, he clearly says that he thought Jewish people were ruining Germany and that they must not be allowed to be German citizens.

Targets of hatred

Once they were in power the Nazis lost no time in persecuting Jews, beginning with trying to get people not to buy goods from Jews. These Nazis are going round urging German people not to use Jewish shops. In many cases, they also stood guard over the shops, hoping to frighten people away.

Visible camps

While some camps, like death camps, were hidden from view, many camps, like Plaszów shown here, were close enough to towns for the townspeople to have known that there was a camp there and to have seen the prisoners.

Who knew?

No one in Nazi-controlled countries could have been in any doubt that the Nazis hated and persecuted Jewish people. However, people disagree over how much ordinary people knew about what went on in the camps and during the **Holocaust**. Historians immediately after the war often suggested that most people knew nothing about the Holocaust and that the Nazis kept what went on secret. Some later historians have suggested the exact opposite – that almost everyone knew. It is more likely that different people knew different things, depending on where they lived. A farming family living well away from any camps or cities, who only read Nazi-approved newspapers and listened to Nazi-run radio, was much less likely to know about the truth of the death camps than a family that lived near a camp.

Who agreed?

Not everyone in Nazi Germany accepted Nazi beliefs, even if they had to seem to agree to stay out of the camps. Some of them even worked secretly against the Nazis. On the other hand there were a lot of people, especially in Germany itself, who were almost hypnotized by the Nazis, and who accepted all Nazi **propaganda** as truth. There were also political groups in other countries that shared Nazi beliefs, including their beliefs about **race**. These groups were happy to **collaborate** with the Nazis.

Different parts of the Reich

The Nazis thought of the land they had taken over in different ways.

- Some places, such as Alsace, which had been made a part of France, were thought of as 'regained' parts of Germany. They were governed as part of Germany.

- Other places, such as parts of pre-war Poland, were to become part of a 'Greater Germany' in time. They were run by German officials. The **Gestapo** and **SS** were sent in to keep order. But the army itself moved out, unless there was fighting on the borders (as in the fighting between Germany and Russia in Poland in 1942–3).

- Finally, there were countries like France or Greece. Neither had ever been part of Germany and both had long histories as separate countries. These countries had to be controlled by the army as well as German officials, the Gestapo (Nazi police) and the SS (who ran the camps).

Nazi ideas

While the countries that the Nazis took over were run differently, some things remained the same. The Nazis tried to introduce their ideas everywhere. They were most successful in Germany itself. They had more difficulty in countries like Denmark and France, both of which had a long history as independent countries. Even then, their success varied. There was a larger group of **anti-Semitic** people in France than in Denmark, for instance, so these people were more likely to accept Nazi anti-Semitism. However, this does not mean the French were more likely to accept Nazi rule. Their resistance movements fought the German occupation just as fiercely as the Danish resistance.

Heil Hitler!

This is part of a crowd at a Nazi rally in Germany in 1938. They are shouting *'Heil Hitler!'* and giving the Nazi salute. Hitler and the Nazis demanded that people accept and obey Nazi ideals. They called this acceptance of Nazi ideas *Gleichschaltung*, meaning that everyone looked at life in the same way.

The family

The Nazis saw families as important. They thought that men should work and fight, while women should care for the home and raise lots of strong, healthy children. This photograph shows an 'ideal' Nazi family. The father is in the SS. The mother has lots of children, girls and boys. Everyone is healthy and well fed.

Obedience

The most important Nazi idea, and the one they enforced most harshly, was obedience to the state. People were constantly told that their convenience, comfort and even safety were less important than that of Germany. As early as 1933, official Nazi documents clearly stated: 'It is all very well to reward people's merits, but the welfare of the nation must come first.' The Nazis expected people to make sacrifices for their country and leader. If a member of their family was not behaving properly, it was their duty to report that person to the block warden, the Nazi official in charge of their area.

The block warden

The Nazis clearly laid out the duties of a block warden. This description comes from the notes a Nazi official made for a lecture:

'The block consists of 40–60 families. The most important function of a block warden is the house visit. Every house is to be visited at least once a month, so the block warden will need assistants, one for every 10 households. The block warden needs to be aware of: the political views of the family; how committed the family is to work and to the Party; any way in which the family might influence other families; the worries, wishes and needs of the family.'

Nazi organizations

A 'good German' was expected to join one of the many different Nazi organizations. If they did not, then the block warden would arrive to ask why not. Not everyone wanted to join and some refused. However, 'good Germans' then treated them with suspicion, which could be dangerous.

Dangerous to joke?

An anti-Nazi joke told in Germany criticized the way that Nazi organizations took over peoples' lives:

> '"My father is in the **SA**, my elder brother is in the SS, my younger brother is in the Hitler Youth, my mother is in the National Socialist Women's League and I am in the League of German Maidens."

> "But how do you ever have time to get together with all these meetings?"

> "Oh we meet once a year at the Nazi Party Rally in Nuremberg!"'

From 1940 the punishment for telling an anti-Nazi joke was hanging.

Propaganda

The Nazis believed that they would have to enforce their ideas at first, but that eventually people would follow them on their own. They used propaganda to make this happen. They made sure that the only ideas that were discussed on radio or in newspapers and magazines were Nazi ideas. They put up posters everywhere pushing their ideas. Irene Gut Opdyke, a young Polish nurse, remembers the German arrival in Radom, Poland:

> 'Posters were pasted to the walls – cruel, mocking posters – linking the Jews to every sin. All the troubles of the Poles were laid at their feet. Loudspeakers on street corners blared warnings about the Jews in Polish and German.'

Taking over other countries

The Germans used **blitzkrieg** tactics because speed was important in invading a country. If they attacked swiftly, the army had to do less fighting because the other countries were slower to gather their armies. The less fighting the German army had to do, the fewer the casualties and the less war supplies were used up. Once the army had taken over a country, the Gestapo and SS arrived to keep control. The Nazis found that the quicker they took over, the better. People were still shocked and had little time to organize resistance. Tomi Ungerer, now a writer and illustrator, was a boy when the Germans took over Alsace:

'The Germans didn't just arrive; they marched in, closely followed by their field kitchen. It was so quick. The French soldiers stationed in Logelbach vanished overnight and the Germans marched in. In the nearest town, Colmar, the commander of the invading unit at once demanded 2300 kg of bread, 557 kg of sausages, 290 kg of butter, 7 kg of tea, 23 kg of coffee, 290 litres of rum, 23,000 packets of cigarettes and 20 civil servants as hostages.'

'Germanization'

One result of the Nazi takeover was the 'Germanization' of the country. Local people soon found that they had to learn German, fast. They needed it to be able to deal with German officials and police – German speakers were more likely to be seen as 'useful'. Even people sent to a concentration camp found speaking German helpful. They were more likely to get an 'easy' job in a camp office. Germanization did not just involve making the locals learn the German language. Street names were translated into German and German laws were quickly introduced.

13

Working for Germany

It was expected that all the countries in the German **Reich** would produce goods and raw materials for Germany first and their own people second. Hitler made it quite clear in several speeches and conversations that: 'It is impossible for Germany to produce everything we need. So we must capture the countries with things we need, especially those things we need to continue the war.' The Reich Economics Minister, Walther Funk, had to produce a plan under which Germany could take food, goods and workers from any of the countries it controlled. In 1939, Germany had 301,000 foreign workers. This rose rapidly and by 1944 the Reich had 7,126,000 foreign workers. This figure does not include slave labour from people in labour camps and concentration camps.

Since occupied countries had to work for Germany, it meant that despite being at war, Germany became one of the better off European nations. However, this

Putting Germany first

The people of Paris had to pay to feed and house the German soldiers and horses shown in this photo. They also had to pay to keep German weapons in good working order.

improvement in the German economy came at a price. Schemes to reduce unemployment and poverty meant that workers were better off, but they were no longer allowed to form unions to protect their rights. The unemployed or homeless ended up in camps.

Papers

Everyone in Nazi-controlled land needed documents to prove their identity, documents to prove whether or not they were **Aryan**, and work documents. People needed documents to travel in their own country and even more documents to leave it. Men of the right age to serve in the army needed either army documents or documents that explained why they were not in the army. All these documents were called 'papers' for short. Anyone could have their papers checked, at any time.

Anti-Semitism

Wherever they went, the Nazis began to persecute local Jewish people as soon as they arrived. They put up anti-Semitic posters, and radios and loudspeakers churned out anti-Jewish propaganda. There was often very little gap between the start of German occupation and the herding up of Jewish people to be sent to concentration camps.

The Germans marched into Alsace in France on 17 June 1940. They took control and began to spread Nazi ideas at once. One of their first propaganda moves was against Jewish people. Many Jews had decided to leave Alsace as soon as the Germans moved in. Those who moved quickly got away to safety. Those who tried to sell their homes, and make other arrangements that took time, were less lucky. By 16 July the Nazis were ready to make Alsace **Judenfrei**. Notices appeared telling all Jews to pack a suitcase and enough food for five days. They were to be sent to France, to temporary transit camps, before being sent to camps in Eastern Europe. They were allowed to take 2000 francs with them, but no jewellery – not even wedding rings.

Life in Hitler's Europe

Life across Hitler's Europe had a pattern of Nazi control. However, people led very different lives. How rich or what race you were, the country you lived in, even if you could speak German – all these things affected your life. Two workers in a factory with similar lives before the Nazis came to power could have very different lives after, especially if one was Jewish. If the non-Jew was a 'good German', who believed in Nazi ideas, his living conditions might well improve under the Nazis. His Jewish co-worker would be lucky to survive Nazi rule.

Local differences

One of the biggest differences in the way that countries sucked into the Reich reacted to Nazi ideas was in how they persecuted Jewish people. In Hungary, most persecution of Jews was done by Arrow-Cross Party 'officers', as shown here. The Arrow Cross was a Hungarian organization that held many of the same beliefs as the Nazi Party.

Life for children

The **Nazis** thought children were very important – they were the future. So the Nazis tried to make sure that all children in the **Reich** learned to love Adolf Hitler and the Nazi state. Even colouring books for pre-school children included the **swastika** symbol.

Schools

The Nazis wanted schools to teach children how to be good Nazis. The Minister of Education said: 'The whole aim of education is to create Nazis.' The first step was to make sure all teachers were good Nazis. 'Unreliable' teachers, who did not support Nazi ideas, were sacked. Teachers were forced to join the National Socialist Teachers' League if they wanted to keep their jobs.

The National Socialist Teacher's League held regular 'Teachers' Camps' on what to teach and how to teach it. Children, the League said: 'must no longer be allowed to choose how to grow up. They must be taught the ideas we know to be right: the ideas of National Socialism.' The Nazis set the subjects taught in schools and chose the textbooks. All this made it almost impossible for teachers to do anything but teach Nazi **propaganda** or stop teaching altogether.

School curriculum

Schools were supposed to make sure that children grew into the kind of people the Nazis wanted. So school subjects, and their importance in the timetable, was tied to producing good soldiers, workers and mothers. The timetable below shows a typical week's lessons at a girls' school in Nazi Germany.

Periods	Monday	Tuesday	Wednesday	Thursday	Friday	Saturday
8:00–8:45	German	German	German	German	German	German
8:50–9:35	Geography	History	Singing	Geography	History	Singing
9:40–10:25	Race Study	Race Study	Race Study	Ideology	Ideology	Ideology
10:25–11:00	Recess, with sports and special announcements					
11:00–12:05	Domestic science with mathematics, every day					
12:10–12:55	Health Biology/Eugenics (see glossary), alternating					

'Jew free' schools

At first, **Jewish** children were allowed to stay in ordinary schools, although they were bullied and used as 'teaching aids' in race studies. Ursula Rosenfeld, a Jewish girl living in a small town near Hamburg, remembers:

> 'Suddenly, no one would share a desk with me. I had to sit in a corner, at the back, on my own. When they had race studies I had to stand outside in the corridor. When I went back into class I could feel the tension. Everyone was staring, looking at you as if you were vermin.'

Jewish children and teachers were soon banned from ordinary schools. This picture from a children's book shows a Jewish teacher and Jewish pupils being thrown out of a school to make it **Judenfrei** – 'Jew free'.

Shaping minds

The Nazis were not concerned about giving children a good education. They wanted them to be turned into good Nazis. Teachers made it clear to even the youngest children that their first duty was to the state. If, for instance, they suspected anyone in their family of being anti-Nazi, they had to report them at once. Teachers also had to teach new subjects covering Nazi ideas that were clearly wrong. So, school timetables now had subjects like '**race** studies', which taught children that the people of the world were divided into racial groups, depending on who their ancestors were long ago, and that Germans belonged to the best race, the **Aryan** race. There was a lot more P.E. to make sure everyone was fit and healthy. Girls had a lot of 'domestic science' in their timetables. This taught them to cook, iron and bring up babies.

Propaganda in schools

Children were bombarded with Nazi propaganda, even in ordinary subjects at school, like maths and science. Here is a question from a maths textbook (RM = Reichmarks, German money):

> 'It costs 4 RM a day to keep a mentally ill person. A civil servant earns 4 RM a day. There are at least 300,000 people in mental asylums at the moment.
>
> a) How much do they cost the state each day?
>
> b) How many marriage loans [money the government lent to 'good Germans' to marry and set up a home] of 1000 RM could the government pay out each day if they did not have to care for the mentally ill?'

17

Youth groups

The Nazis also set up various Hitler Youth groups for children to join. They were divided up by sex and age (boys and girls were both in groups aged 10–14 or 14–18). They all stressed loyalty to the state and Adolf Hitler and provided lots of physical exercise, competition and patriotic singing. These groups held meetings after school, in the evening and at weekends. They also took children away on holidays, usually walking and camping out. By the end of 1933, about a third of all German children aged 10–18 were in the Hitler Youth.

Tightening their hold

At first, children did not have to join Hitler Youth groups. After 1936 there was a lot of pressure to join; almost two thirds had joined by the end of 1937. In 1939 a law was passed saying they had to join. If they did not join a group, their parents were fined or put in prison. In countries that Germany took over in Western Europe, children could not go to school unless they were members of the Hitler Youth.

Getting used to a uniform

The Nazis insisted that all Hitler Youth groups wore a uniform like this and learned to obey orders. It was especially important for boys, as later they were expected to serve in the army. Nazi posters from the time (behind the uniform) made this connection clear.

The Hitler Youth Promise

The Hitler Youth Promise talked about Hitler, who was the Führer (leader), and the **Reich** in an almost religious way. This was not accidental. The Nazis wanted people to follow Hitler and believe in him as if he was a god:

'You, *Führer*, are our commander!
We stand in your name.
The Reich is what we fight for,
It is the beginning and the Amen.

Your word is the heartbeat of our deeds;
Your faith builds cathedrals for us.
And even when death reaps
    the last harvest
The crown of the Reich never falls.

We are ready, your silent spell
Makes us one, forms us into
An iron chain, man beside man,
Into a wall of loyalty around you.'

Young resistance

The Nazis were concerned about groups, like the Edelweiss Pirates or the Navajo gang, which actively fought Hitler Youth groups. Once Germany was at war and the Hitler Youth gave up almost all activities for military training, more young people left the Hitler Youth and joined other groups. One Edelweiss Pirate said:

> 'It was the Hitler Youth's own fault I left. It changed so all we did was march and every order I was given came with a threat.'

Once war broke out, some gangs also worked with resistance movements to fight the Nazis and help Allied troops and people who had escaped from prisons, camps and **ghettos** to get out of German-controlled land. The photo shows older members of the Edelweiss Pirates group in Cologne who were caught helping resistance movements. The Nazis hanged anyone found doing this, no matter how young they were.

All in favour?

Even inside Germany itself there were some young people who did not join the Hitler Youth. Some even formed groups opposing Nazi ideas. Groups called 'swing' groups listened to American music and dressed very casually. This might not sound like much of a rebellion, but in Nazi Germany it was a crime. As fast as the Nazis stamped out groups, new groups sprang up. In 1942 the Reich Youth Leadership admitted: 'The formation of groups of young people outside the Hitler Youth has been increasing since the outbreak of war.' The most worrying thing for the Nazis was that, by 1942, nearly all young people had been through the Nazi school system. Yet there were still some who did not blindly accept Nazi beliefs. This meant that Nazi propaganda was clearly not a total success.

Playtime

The Nazis encouraged different roles for men and women. They thought men should work to earn a living and serve as soldiers. Women were expected to stay at home, look after the family and house and have lots of children. So, children were encouraged to play with the 'right sort' of toys. Girls were given tea sets, dolls and prams to practise being a housewife. Boys played with toy soldiers like the one shown here, to prepare them for when they became a soldier.

German families

Schools and youth groups took up a lot of children's time, but they still had some family life. The Nazis encouraged big families. They also encouraged extended families, where grandparents lived in the home. This was to stress the importance of a person's ancestors, to remind children of how important it was to come from a long line of people with 'pure' German blood.

Large families

The Nazis wanted 'good Germans' to have a lot of children, to settle in the countries Germany was taking over and Germanize them. The Nazis lent suitable couples 1000 Reichmarks (RM) when they married to help set up a home. The Nazis cut the loan by 250 RM for every child they had. Having four children meant the parents had nothing to repay. The Nazis also cut taxes for large families and gave them cheap train fares, school fees and holidays. This help was not given to families outside Germany. It had the effect the Nazis wanted. More people married and families got bigger. Children in Nazi Germany were likely to have many brothers and sisters.

A busy life

The Nazis saw spending time alone as **asocial**. Children in German families were encouraged to lead busy lives. They were either in school, or ***kindergarten*** for those under six years old, or at youth group meetings. Youth groups also organized other activities, like collecting for charities. Children had to help in the home, too. This help depended on their age and where they lived. Farmers' children helped on the farm from a very young age.

Families outside Germany

Families outside Germany were not treated as well as 'good' German families, but they did not have to follow as many rules either. Women were discouraged from working and children were expected to join Hitler Youth groups. Otherwise, family life could carry on as normal, as long as people obeyed the new Nazi laws. Children from families the Nazis saw as asocial or **undesirable** were taken away from their parents, or sent with them to **concentration camps**.

Unwanted children

When they imprisoned and killed Jewish people, babies, young children and pregnant mothers were among the first to die. This was partly because they could not work efficiently. It was also because children were the next generation – they gave people hope and carried on a race that the Nazis wanted to wipe out. Disabled German children were also killed. Women considered 'unsuitable' as mothers because of their race or a disability were operated on to stop them having children.

'Aryanizing' children

When the Nazis took over Poland, they took young Polish children that looked Aryan away from their parents. They sent the children for adoption to German families who could not have children. The Nazis thought that with 'better' parents these children would become good Nazis. The younger a child, the easier it was for them to settle quickly. The boy in this photo is the kind of child the Nazis chose, although his age would mean he might settle more slowly. The Nazis did not separate families in Western Europe in this way, because they saw the people in these countries as more civilized.

Making friends

Making friends in Hitler's Europe was difficult. Children couldn't just make friends with someone they liked. Children, or their parents if they were young children, had to think about how suitable another child was. It was dangerous to make the wrong sort of friend. It was especially dangerous for children with something to hide. If you were Jewish, but pretending not to be, or if your parents were working against the Nazis, it was dangerous to make friends with someone from a Nazi family. Children did not always understand that if they said something to the wrong person it could be a disaster. Christabel Bielenberg, an Englishwoman living in Germany, remembers:

> 'My son, Nicky, came home from school one day after playing with his friend Werner. "Do you know Werner's mother listens to the radio like you do, with her ear right up against it?" he asked. [This meant they were listening to a banned radio station – a crime that earned at least five years in prison and could get a person hung.]
> "She's probably a bit deaf, like me," I said firmly.'

Losing old friends

Once the Nazis came to power, many Jewish children found that it was hard to stay friends with non-Jews. Anne Fox, a Jewish girl living in Berlin, remembers the effect of the Nazis coming to power on her friendships:

> 'My friend Tuke, who lived in the same apartment block, came to play less and less often. My mother didn't like me going up to their apartment, either. Tuke's older brother, Hans, was in the **SA** and her father was one of the first to join the **SS**. The boys marched and sang, with all the other Nazis: "When Jewish blood spurts from the knife, how much better everything will be!" How could a friendship cope with that?'

Safety in numbers

Children in Nazi Germany were encouraged to make large groups of friends in their Hitler Youth groups. This meant that friendships were less deep and less likely to affect a child's loyalty to the Nazis. These girls are at a Hitler Youth camp for 14–18 year olds.

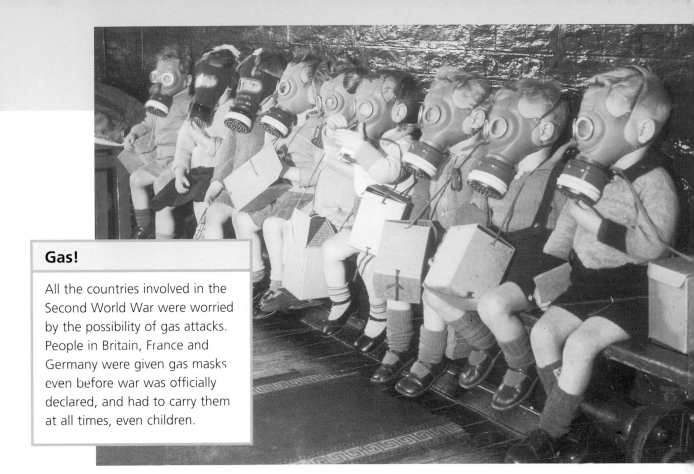

War!

Germany was at war with various other countries from 1939–45, including Britain and France from 1939, and the Soviet Union and the USA from 1941. This affected all the children living in Germany and occupied Europe. Many German families were broken up as fathers and elder brothers had to join the army. Many city children were sent away from their homes when bombing raids on Germany began. They did not have to go, but there was a lot of pressure on parents to send their children. They were safer in the countryside, but it was another change to get used to. Children aged 6–10 were sent to live with families. Children aged 10–14 were sent to live in state-organized hostels or campsites.

Rationing

The Nazis rationed food, petrol, fuel and clothes from August 1939, the month before war broke out. This meant Germans were only allowed a certain amount of all these things. Often, it was not nearly as much as people had been used to. Children in all the countries affected by the war were affected by shortages of food and other everyday things.

Starving in the ghettos

Jewish children who were herded with their families into **ghettos** suffered from rationing more than other children. The Nazis only let a small amount of food into the ghetto – less than enough to keep everyone alive. People died every day in every ghetto from starvation.

Life for women

The **Nazis** had strong ideas about the role of women. They wanted women to marry, run the home and have lots of children. They did not want women, especially married women, to work. As the war took away more and more men to fight, the Nazis had to change their views about working women and ask them to do war work for their country. But they made it clear that they wanted this to be a temporary, emergency, change.

Bombing

This photo shows women clearing away the rubble in Berlin after a British bombing raid in 1945. The British and Germans bombed each other's cities heavily between 1941 and 1945. Hermine Jundt, a young mother living in Mannheim, wrote to a friend:

'Things are so awful here now, Anna. Thirteen bombs dropped near us. They've made huge craters and the dirt and rubble are awful. When we got home from the shelter I wanted to howl. No lights, no water, no gas! I didn't know where to begin. Over 180,000 firebombs were dropped on the town, so you can imagine that the fires were burning for days on end.'

Bringing up a family

Hitler said in a speech in 1934: 'Equal rights for women means valuing them for the job nature has given them.' He believed that men and women were made differently and had different skills. Both sets of skills were needed for a state to work well. One of the jobs only women could do was having babies and bringing up the next generation of German citizens. This meant valuing mothers. Mothers in Nazi Germany were given extra rations and were even given medals for having a lot of healthy babies. Anna Klein, a young German mother who lived in Vienna, remembers:

'Ever since I was little all I had wanted was to be a mother and have lots of babies. I really fitted Hitler's image of the perfect German mother. I felt lucky to be a mother then, too. I was treated as if I was special, not like my mother and aunties had been – they didn't get all those extras.'

Feeding a family

Feeding a family became harder and harder with wartime rationing, especially in the cities. People had coupons that they swapped for their rations, as shown in the photograph. But just because people had the coupons did not mean that they got the food. One woman remembered:

'You spent all morning shopping for food. The queues were terrible. And you had to queue over and over, for each thing, bread, meat, groceries. It could be heartbreaking. Sometimes, if you were late getting to the shops, the shopkeepers ran out just as you got to the front of the queue, over and over.'

Women living in the countryside could keep hens for eggs, and to eat when they stopped laying. Some local farmers sold or swapped spare milk, butter or cheese.

Foreign women

Non-German women living in Germany were treated with suspicion. Christabel Bielenberg, an Englishwoman married to a German, found that she was treated with suspicion in Berlin, but people were more friendly when she moved to the countryside. The Nazis did not force the women of occupied Europe to behave like German women, but they did not give them any of the benefits, either.

A different attitude?

Many women who worked in resistance movements remembered that it was an advantage being a woman, especially a pretty young woman. A Polish resister remembers: 'I smiled and flirted with the Nazi guards. These were my weapons.' They deliberately tried to fit the Nazi image and used this to appear invisible. This did not help them if they were caught helping the resistance. They were hung.

Working life

Before the **Nazis** took over, Germany, like much of the rest of Europe, had serious economic problems. High unemployment and rising prices made it hard for many people to make a living.

Improvements

The Nazis took jobs away from **Jews** and women and gave them to 'suitable' unemployed German men. The next unemployment figures did not count Jews or women – and so dropped hugely. The Nazis set up state work projects, building roads and re-building cities, creating nearly 2 million more jobs for men who accepted Nazi rule. Wages began to go up, while prices stopped going up so quickly. Nazi organizations made sure working conditions were good and provided free sporting activities and cheap holidays. The Nazis also helped unemployed people who they thought were genuinely unable to work by providing for their basic needs. However, unemployed people who the Nazis thought were avoiding work were described as **asocial** and sent to the camps.

Hard work

The Nazis believed that hard physical work was good for people and produced fit, healthy **citizens**. Young people in Nazi-controlled lands were expected to spend six months doing Labour Service as soon as they were eighteen years old. This work usually involved making roads or working on farms. These postcards show young men happily 'working for Germany'.

More restrictions

Only men who accepted Nazi ideas were likely to find their working life improved. Many **undesirable** people lost their jobs under the Nazis. Also, workers could not set up their own trade unions to say what they wanted. Trade unions were banned and many of their leaders were sent to **concentration camps**. Working conditions were hard, as Ernst Bromberg, a steelworks fitter, remembers:

'There was no time to get into politics when you were working three shifts with the Labour Front breathing down your necks. You got up, went to work, didn't overstretch your breaks and took the money. It was good money.'

Forced to work

People in countries to the east of Germany, such as Poland, were forced to work. The Nazis classed people in these eastern countries as Slavs. To the Nazis, Slavs were *untermenschen* – less than human, so the Nazis did not treat them as if they had human rights. If the Nazis in Radom, for instance, needed workers for a factory, they simply went out with trucks and loaded up healthy-looking Poles from the street. These people were not allowed to collect any things or to tell their families they were going. Irene Gut Opdyke, a young Polish girl, was taken from a church in Radom:

'The soldiers began dividing people up and I was dragged to a group of "fit workers". Three trucks roared into the church square and we were chased into them. We were driven to some kind of camp, surrounded by barbed wire. "You will be taken to Germany to work for the **Reich**," an officer told us. "You Poles have been idle long enough."'

Germany first

Workers in occupied Western Europe were not as badly treated as in Eastern Europe, but they still had to put Germany first. Despite claiming that all the countries were working for a common goal, the Nazis were actually exploiting Europe. Farmers had their food taken to feed the German army. Factories were re-equipped to make ammunition and other goods for Germany's war.

Leisure time

The **Nazis** wanted people to work hard for Hitler and Germany. By the time they had done their work and gone to all the meetings of groups they had to join, people had very little free time left. However, the Nazis encouraged suitable group entertainment, which they used to spread Nazi **propaganda**. They built cinemas and theatres to show Nazi-approved films and plays. The Nazis also made cheap radios and gave many of them away to poor families who would otherwise not be able to afford one. This meant that, as a poster of the time said: 'Everyone listens to the *Führer* on National Radio!'

Culture

Herman Goering, a member of the Nazi Party and a close friend of Hitler, summed up many Nazis' attitude when he said: 'Whenever I hear the word "culture" I reach for my revolver.' But Hitler wanted the world to see the Nazis as cultured, not thugs. So, the Nazis supported painters, musicians, writers and playwrights – as long as they supported Nazi ideas. Everyone else was '**degenerate**' and their works were banned. The last thing the Nazis wanted was people being encouraged to think for themselves. They held regular public burnings of 'degenerate' books. The first of these was on 10 May 1933, after they had been in power for under four months.

The 1936 Olympic Games

In 1936 Germany hosted the Olympic Games. Hitler had a brand new Olympic Stadium built for the Games. This was the Nazis' chance to show the world how 'civilized' they were, how much better their **Aryan** athletes were than other athletes. The streets were cleaned of their most violent anti-Jewish posters and obvious violence against Jews and other '**undesirables**' was discouraged. It was a great humiliation for Hitler to watch while a black American athlete, Jesse Owens, won four gold medals, beating Aryan athletes. Hitler ignored Owens and walked out when the crowd stood to cheer his win in the 200 metres sprint. Out of 129 events, Germany won only 33 gold medals.

BERLIN 1936
1–16 AUG.

OLYMPISCHE SPIELE

A fan of Mickey Mouse

Hitler saw his first Mickey Mouse cartoon in 1937. He loved it so much that the propaganda minister, Joseph Goebbels, gave him twelve Mickey cartoons for Christmas. Goebbels set up a team of over 100 cartoonists to study and copy Disney's techniques to make propaganda films such as *The Jewish Rhinoceros*, a frame of which is shown here. In it, a Jewish rhinoceros exploits all the other animals for his own profit and has to be defeated. Goebbels wanted to be able to use them to spread propaganda in any country that Germany took over, subtitling them in a variety of languages.

Shakespeare – a good German?

The Nazis tried to prove that anyone who had invented anything useful, or written or composed anything important, was really German. The English playwright, William Shakespeare, had been important in Germany for many years. The Nazis did not want to ban Shakespeare at once, for fear of upsetting too many people. Instead they had editions of his plays 're-edited' to smooth away anything anti-Nazi. The Ministry of Propaganda even wrote a pamphlet called *Shakespeare – a Germanic Writer*. Then, in 1939, Germany went to war with Britain and all 'enemy dramatists' were banned. Hitler, who liked Shakespeare, said he was not banned. So Nazi propaganda showed Shakespeare as a writer only Germans understood – the British were too stupid: 'The only Shakespeare known in England today is a football player of that name.' However, one by one the plays came to be seen as 'unacceptable'. In the end, the Nazis put so many restrictions on which plays could be performed, and how many times, that they might as well have banned them.

Undermining religion, creating suspicion

Hitler realized that the **Nazis** could not just ban all religions. Too many people had sincerely held beliefs for this to have any chance of success. So when the Nazis came to power, Hitler was friendly to the Christian Church. He even made an agreement with the Pope that the Nazis would not interfere with the Catholic Church as long as the Pope did not interfere in German politics.

Undermining the churches

However, Hitler secretly worked against the Catholic Church, which said Catholics should obey the Pope before the ruler of their country. The Nazis never banned the Catholic Church, but they persecuted Catholic priests. They set up the 'German Christian Church', with the aim of: 'embracing all the people into a National Socialist State... One Nation! One God! One **Reich**! One Church!' They also encouraged 'nature worship'. So, they celebrated Easter as the old spring festival to undermine the traditional Christian festival. Outside Germany, the Nazis allowed Christians to go on worshipping in their own way.

The Jewish faith

There was one religion the Nazis never tolerated – the **Jewish** faith. Jewish synagogues were often targets of Nazi violence. On the night of 9 November 1938 the Nazis carried out a planned, countrywide attack against Jews, known as *Kristallnacht* (Night of Broken Glass) because of all the damage done. Over a thousand synagogues were burned down and many more were looted. Eric Lucas, a Jewish boy living in Aachen, remembers:

> 'Three men threw the scrolls of the Law of Moses [part of the Jewish sacred writings] to the screaming mass of people. The people caught the scrolls and tossed them as if playing a ball game. They were torn and trampled.'

Moving around

Under the Nazis it was not possible for anyone to move around freely, especially after war broke out in 1939. Walking or bicycling short distances were the quickest ways to get around, although you might have to show your papers at any time. Train travel needed a permit and, from 1939 on, was likely to be difficult and dangerous because of the war.

'Suspicious' people

The Nazis encouraged people to report anyone 'suspicious', who might, for instance, be listening to British radio broadcasts, or hiding Jewish families. The Nazis were quick to imprison people for anything, especially foreign men. Any foreigners who had a job where they could pass on anti-Nazi views were almost automatically seen as opponents and arrested, as in the case of Stefan Lorant. Before the war, if they were lucky, they simply went to prison until they could be sent out of Germany. After the war had started they were sent to concentration camps.

Stefan Lorant – under arrest

Stefan Lorant was a Hungarian filmmaker and photographer. He was arrested in Munich on 14 March 1933, just five days after the Nazis took over in Bavaria. He was kept in Munich prison for six and a half months, and constantly shifted from cell to cell, always fearing he might be executed or sent to a concentration camp, as other **politicals** had been. The worst thing was the uncertainty. Eventually the Hungarian embassy managed to get him released. He was given a day to leave the country and return to Hungary. In Britain, in 1935, he published his book, *I was Hitler's Prisoner*. In this he said:

'For six and a half months I was in "**protective custody**" as a political offender. Why? I was never told. My case never came to trial. My wife, by trying to get me released, upset the political police. She was imprisoned for six and a half weeks, also with no explanation and no trial.'

Life in the ghettos

Ghettos were places, usually parts of cities or towns, where the **Nazis** forced **Jewish** people to live. Cramming Jews into ghettos made the rest of the city and the land around it *Judenfrei* –'Jew free'. The first ghetto was set up in Piotrkow, Poland, in October 1939. Gradually they were set up in many other cities. The largest of these were in Warsaw and Lodz.

A good thing?

At first, many Jewish people welcomed the setting up of ghettos. There were several reasons for this. Ghettos had been set up from medieval times onwards, so they were familiar. The people in these ghettos had lived separately, but they had still lived normal lives. They had been allowed to move around outside the ghettos and do business with non-Jews. So the Jews hoped that the Nazi ghettos would work in the same way. Also, there was less obvious persecution at first, because there was less contact with non-Jews. It looked as though things would settle down, rather than carry on getting worse. Everyone in the ghetto was Jewish and a *Judenrat*, Jewish Council, was set up to run things. Jewish people would be cut off from the outside world, but running things for themselves.

It soon became clear that the Nazis ghettos would not be like earlier ones. The Nazi ghettos were walled and guarded parts of cities and towns into which Jews were crammed firstly from the Polish countryside and then from Germany and other lands occupied by Germany.

The Warsaw ghetto

This photograph was taken in the Warsaw ghetto in 1940, not long after the ghetto had been set up. The streets are crowded, but people are still reasonably well fed and do not yet look to be starving.

All together

Ghettos crammed a lot of people into a small area – and numbers went on rising as the Nazis rounded up more and more Jews. About 500,000 people were forced into the Warsaw ghetto. Despite the fact that they died at rates that varied from 1000 to 6000 a month, the ghetto population rose as the Nazis crammed more and more Jews from Germany, occupied Europe and Poland into it. The same thing happened in the other ghettos.

The advantages that many Jews had hoped for did not happen. The *Judenrat* had to obey the Nazis, so Jews were not running their own lives. The ghetto held Jewish people in one place, so the Nazis knew just where to find them to persecute them. The Nazis regularly cut off water and electricity supplies, using the excuse of wartime 'rationing'. They limited supplies of food and medicine.

Propaganda comes true

This photo shows the entrance to the Jewish ghetto in Radom. The notice outside warns against entry 'because of disease'. By cramming people into the ghettos in the way that they did, with limited access to water, medicine, heat and electricity, the Nazis made sure that their **propaganda** about Jews being dirty and carrying diseases came true. People in the ghetto made huge efforts to stay clean and to help the sick, but they were fighting such terrible conditions that they were sure to lose.

In 1941 the ration for a German adult was 2613 calories (approximately the recommended daily calorie intake today). Poles were only allowed 699 calories. Jews in the ghettos got 184 calories – well below the amount needed to survive. The overcrowding and lack of water, heat and light soon led to the rapid spread of disease.

Isolated

Because Jewish people were cut off in ghettos it was easier for the Nazis to persecute them and for people outside the ghetto to ignore this. The Nazis were forcing people in the ghetto to live in appalling conditions – but they exaggerated even these conditions to make Jewish people seem inhuman. The **SS** paper, *Das Schwarze Korps*, said in an article on ghettos in 1939:

> 'The ghetto is unbelievably filthy, a maze of alleys and overfilled buildings, full of Jews whose numbers increase rapidly, despite poverty and typhus. Countless habitual criminals, murderers, swindlers and pickpockets hide here – they have to be cleared out of their underground rats' nests by German cleaning crews at the risk of their own lives. This clearing strains the nerves of the men who have to fight through the stench, muck, muck and more muck, through vermin-infested and disgusting Jewish living spaces.'

Work break

These Jewish workers in the Lodz ghetto have stopped for a meal break. The factories fed the workers a thin soup in the middle of the day. It was often the only food they had all day, despite the heavy work and long hours.

Equality in the ghetto

Not everyone in the ghetto was equal. Members of the *Judenrat* and Jews who had been wealthy before the Nazi occupation lived far better than other people. People who ran the ghetto workshops also had better lives. This meant they had their own flats with electricity and running water, rather than having to share. They were given more food.

The poor people sent to the ghetto well after the ghetto was set up ended up the worst off. They lived in the poorest parts of the ghetto, with several families forced to share a single room that had no water, heat or light.

Deportations

In 1942 the Nazis decided that it was not enough for Jews to be left in the ghetto to die of disease and starvation. It was not even enough to put them in the camps and work them to death. Special death camps were set up to do nothing but kill Jewish people and other **undesirables** such as the Gypsies.

Jews in the ghetto were ferried to these camps by train, having been told they would be 'resettled' outside German land. It was suspicious that the first to go were the very young, the old, the sick and the pregnant – not healthy people who could have set up a settlement. As trainload after trainload of people left and small ghettos were 'liquidated', it became harder to believe that the trains were taking people to anything but their death. People in the ghettos began to revolt against the Nazis.

The Terezín ghetto

In October 1941, the Nazis decided to turn the walled town of Terezín, in Czechoslovakia, into a ghetto. They moved all the non-Jewish people out and, over the next few months, moved about 40,000 Jewish people in. Terezín was unusual in that the Nazis used it as a 'model' ghetto to show that conditions in ghettos were not bad. They filmed it in 1944 and even showed members of the Red Cross charity organization around it, having first carried out an 'improvement action' to make it look far better than it was. An SS man drove the leader of the *Judenrat*, Paul Eppstein, around the ghetto in a car. The same SS man had beaten Eppstein up the day before, and would do so again.

An unknown destination

These people are being loaded on to trains leaving the Lodz ghetto in the summer of 1944. They were told they were being sent to settle lands further east, setting up new Jewish communities. In fact, they were being sent to death camps.

The Lodz ghetto

We are going to look at life in the Lodz **ghetto** in more detail. The Lodz ghetto was set up in April 1940. The **Jewish** people of Lodz hardly fitted into the ghetto, let alone all the people from the nearby countryside too. In the first month or so about 38,000 Jews were sent to Lodz. Jews from all over Europe were herded in. Meanwhile, as disease and starvation took hold, the death rate of the people in the ghetto rose rapidly.

Outside contacts

People in other ghettos had some outside contact and some managed to smuggle in money, food or news. Irene Gut Opdyke, a young Polish girl, worked close enough to the Radom ghetto to be able to slip away and sneak food under the ghetto fence each day. The Lodz ghetto was completely cut off. This was partly because there were factories inside Lodz ghetto; Jews did not leave the ghetto to work. But the main reason was that the **Nazis** filled the area around the ghetto with people from Germany, **Aryans** who had no connection with, or sympathy for, the people inside.

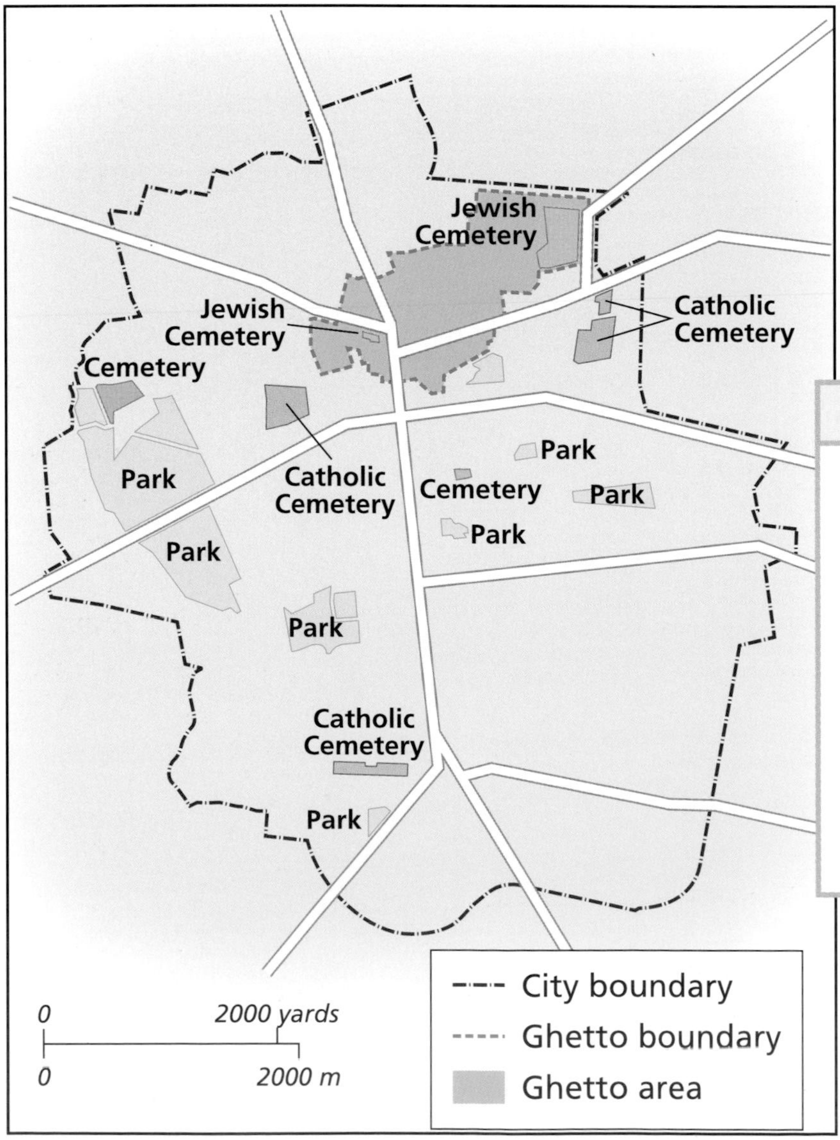

Map labels: Jewish Cemetery, Jewish Cemetery, Cemetery, Catholic Cemetery, Catholic Cemetery, Park, Cemetery, Park, Park, Park, Park, Catholic Cemetery, Park

Scale: 0 — 2000 yards; 0 — 2000 m

Legend:
- –·– City boundary
- ---- Ghetto boundary
- ▨ Ghetto area

The Lodz ghetto

The Lodz ghetto was fenced off with eleven kilometres of barbed wire fence. There were narrow wooden bridges over the 'Aryan' streets. There were 31,721 flats, most of them with only one room and only 725 with running water. Few had an electricity supply. At its fullest, there were over 200,000 people living there.

Finding out about the Lodz ghetto

Survivors from Lodz have talked about their experiences of ghetto life. The *Judenrat* (Jewish Council) that ran the ghetto kept a secret diary of events: *Chronicle of the Lodz Ghetto*. It was written by several people, intended to record exactly what went on. This is the only surviving day-to-day account of events in a ghetto.

The Nazis did not know about the *Chronicle*. The Nazis would have hung the writers, even though they only put down the facts. They did not criticize either the Nazis or the *Judenrat* (whose decisions were not always popular). There are also photos of the ghetto – some taken publicly by Nazi officers and some taken secretly by Jewish photographers.

Mordecai Chaim Rumkowski

This photo shows Mordecai Rumkowski, the leader of the *Judenrat*, at the opening of a new soup kitchen in the Lodz ghetto. Rumkowski was the most well-off man in the ghetto and was often called 'the king'

Running the ghetto

Mordecai Chaim Rumkowski was the leader of the *Judenrat* that ran the Lodz ghetto. He was convinced that the way to survive in the ghetto was to co-operate with the Nazis and show that they were useful. He was sure that if the Jews of the ghetto worked hard for the Nazis they would be allowed to live. He set up offices to run the work, the rationing, schools (Lodz was one of the few ghettos that managed to keep schools going), emergency services and all kinds of welfare. The welfare department organized soup kitchens in various areas and did what they could to look after the poor, old, sick and orphans.

Desperation

Even during the first winter, the lack of food and fuel made people desperate. Coal dust was sold for fuel, while people used whatever they could get as firewood. While some people went out of their way to help others, many people, not surprisingly, put their families first. If they had to steal, they stole. In January 1941 the *Chronicle* reported:

> 'The residents of a building woke today to find that they could not go downstairs. During the night someone had stolen the stairs, banisters and handrail.'

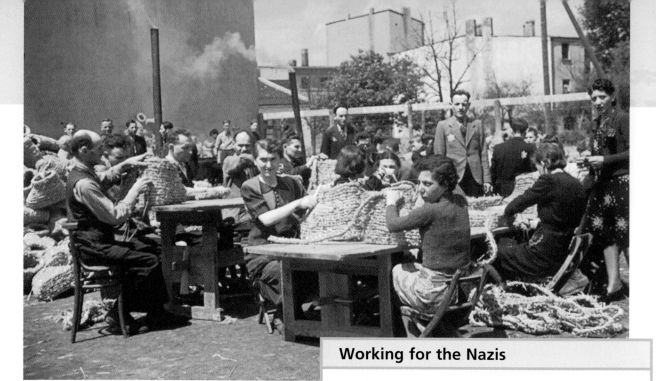

Working for the Nazis

The SS took this colour photo in a ghetto workshop for their records. It made good publicity to show the Red Cross and other concerned organizations. It made it seem that the Jews in the ghettos were being worked hard but not treated too badly.

Work in the ghetto

Everyone in the ghetto worked if they could, for as long as they could. People who worked were fed a meal at their work. Even people who had been doctors or teachers were glad to work many hours a day sweeping floors or clearing rubble.

Good jobs?

Some people were lucky enough to get work running the ghetto. This entitled a person to two bowls of soup a day, not the one that all other workers got. Michael Etkind was a postman in Lodz and remembers that even on two bowls of soup, he was constantly hungry:

> 'We all were. Rations were given out every two weeks. Many people could not stop themselves eating it too quickly. So it was gone by the middle of the second week. So they were so hungry that when the next distribution of bread and butter came they would eat it all too quickly again.'

Some 'official' jobs gave the worker extra rations, but made him unpopular, especially working as a ghetto policeman. The ghetto police had to keep people in the ghetto, carry out Nazi orders and break up the rioting that broke out when conditions were especially bad.

Taken away to work

The Nazis regularly took trainloads of the fittest in the ghetto, usually men, to do forced labour, usually in Germany. They did this before they started deporting people to **concentration camps** and to death camps. On 11 April 1941 they announced that they would take 300 or 400 workers every three or four days for the rest of the month. These men never returned to their families in the ghetto.

Making things worse

The Nazis regularly made things worse in the ghettos, reducing their size while increasing the number of people they crammed in and cutting the amount of food and medicines. In January 1941 the Nazis took a section of the Lodz ghetto away. They did not choose the particular piece of land they took by accident. Their action managed to hit the food supply and increase overcrowding in the ghetto at the same time. The *Chronicle* reported that:

'The 7000 or so people from this area will have to be found somewhere to live. The loss of land is especially painful because the largest fruit and vegetable growing area is there. These were carefully begun last year on land previously used for dumping rubbish.'

Deportations

The Nazis began deportations from Lodz in January 1942. Many people from the Lodz ghetto were taken to Chelmno and Auschwitz-Birkenau death camps. Perec Zylberberg, a young man in the ghetto, remembers:

'The deportations got more and more frequent. We didn't know what was wrong, but we sensed something was. The people in charge were trying so hard to save their relatives from going. I was able to get my mother and sister work at the carpet factory where I worked. Working was a passport to staying on.'

From 23 September 1942 there was a curfew in the ghetto for seven days. Factories were closed, everything stopped and people were collected up for deportation. By the end of the seventh day about 20,000 people were gone. From June to August 1944 the Lodz ghetto was emptied as its residents were transported to death camps. By the time the advancing Russian troops captured Lodz in January 1945, only 870 people remained of the 230,000 in the ghetto at its fullest.

Everyone helps

Very young children did not work in the factories, but they could still help by selling things on street corners. This boy is selling 'homemade sweets'.

Special cases

This chapter looks at the **Nazis**' treatment of three kinds of 'special cases' – people who did not fit into the perfect Nazi state. They are the disabled, the **Gypsies** and **asocials**.

The disabled

In August 1938 the Nazis began to encourage German people to send their disabled relatives to state-run clinics for 'special care'. The clinic at Eglfing-Haar near Munich was one of the first to open. Its director, Dr Hermann Pfannmüller, took some Nazis around in February 1940. One of them remembered:

'He took us into one ward and said: "We have here children from one to five, all living burdens on our nation. We do not poison or inject them – this might give the foreign press a **propaganda** hold against us. No, our way is much simpler." At this he pulled a skeletal child out of one of the cots saying: "Naturally we don't stop all their food at once. That would cause too much fuss. We gradually reduce the portions. Nature takes care of the rest. This one won't last more than two or three days."'

At least 5000 children were killed in this way.

T4

The Nazis had a policy of starving disabled adults, or leaving them exposed in cold weather to freeze to death. They were also mass-gassed by carbon monoxide in an operation codenamed 'T4'. There were six centres for this, like the Hartheim Institute pictured left, scattered all over Germany.

Victims' families got a letter saying the patient had fallen ill:

'...all attempts to keep the patient alive were unfortunately unsuccessful. In accordance with police instructions we had to cremate the corpse at once to prevent spreading infectious disease.'

Gypsies

Gypsies are groups of people who travel together, often on the same routes year after year, meeting up in larger groups at various times. They share the same language and culture. By the 1930s, some Gypsy families had settled down to live in towns and villages. While some of these people still saw themselves as Gypsies, others did not and some married non-Gypsy people. The Nazis murdered about 300,000 Gypsies in the **Holocaust** that also wiped out millions of **Jews**. Why did the Nazis target the Gypsies?

Racially inferior

The **SS** had orders to treat the Gypsies as if they were Jews: 'to be removed from Europe as an inferior race'. The Nazis thought it was impossible to re-educate the Gypsies into Nazi ways. Rudolph Hoess, commandant of Auschwitz **concentration camp**, showed this Nazi prejudice when he said: 'Stealing and vagrancy are in their blood and cannot be wiped out.' Nazi officials traced back family lines and arrested people with even a small amount of Gypsy blood. Even Nazi soldiers who did not know they had Gypsy ancestors were sent to Auschwitz.

Travelling people

This photo shows Gypsies in a camp near Hamburg in the spring of 1940. Before they were sent to their deaths, many Gypsies were sent to permanent fenced and guarded campsites like this one. The man in the suit taking notes in the middle of the group is Nazi scientist Dr Robert Ritter, who studied **race**.

Roman Mirga

Roman Mirga's family lived in Warsaw, Poland, working as a Gypsy band. In November 1942, when Roman was 17, they were warned that the Nazis were persecuting Gypsies. The Gypsy leader did not believe they were in danger; then a group of Gypsies vanished and Roman's group fled towards Hungary. They disguised themselves as Polish peasants. The Nazis caught some of them, but some made it, including Roman and his family. When the Germans invaded Hungary, Roman's group were captured and sent to Auschwitz-Birkenau's Gypsy camp. Roman was one of the few kept as workers when 4000 people in the Gypsy camp were gassed on 31 July 1944. Roman and another young Gypsy escaped and hid with a Polish woman until the Russians arrived in January 1945.

Asocials at Hashude

The Nazis wanted healthy **Aryan** asocials, especially families with children, to have a chance to reform. In October 1936 a 'welfare housing institution', called Hashude, was set up in the city of Bremen. It was for 're-educating' asocial families. It looked like an ordinary housing estate, not a prison or a camp. But families were forced to go there, and while there, they were constantly watched.

Constant supervision

The estate at Hashude, shown here, was surrounded by fences and the gates were guarded. The houses had no back doors, just front doors – most of which were overlooked by the Nazi administration building. Welfare officials could go into any house at any time to check what the families were doing, how clean the houses were and how well looked after the children were.

Who was sent to Hashude?

Government Welfare Officials decided which families were sent to Hashude. They chose families that they thought could be changed. Families were chosen if the parents did not work, drank too much, neglected the children or did not pay the rent.

Even members of the Nazi Party could be sent to Hashude. In May 1936 a family was sent to Hashude even though the father had been a member of the Nazi party since it was set up and the children were in Nazi youth groups. The reasons given for sending them there were that the father had not paid the rent for a whole year and his wife's housekeeping showed that 'the ideas of order and cleanliness were unknown to her'.

More freedom

If the welfare officials were satisfied that a family had 'improved' after six months, they were moved to a terraced house and could mix with other families. They had more freedom, although welfare officers could visit at any time. As soon as the officer in charge of Hashude felt that a family was no longer 'a threat to the nation', he reported to the Welfare Authority that they were ready for release. The Welfare Authority then looked for a home for the family and a job for the father. The family were not allowed to leave until these were found.

Hashude closes

In July 1940 Hashude was closed down. A housing shortage in Bremen meant that the houses were too valuable to 'waste' on asocials. The fencing and gates were taken down and it re-opened as ordinary housing for families from Bremen. The Nazis had been rounding up large numbers of asocials and sending them to concentration camps since July 1938. With Hashude gone, there was no other alternative.

The routine in Hashude

In their first six months at Hashude, new families had no contact with other families. Fathers worked in local factories and workshops or did gardening and repairs in Hashude. Mothers looked after the home and children. Houses had to be cleaned by 11 a.m. each day. Welfare officers inspected homes daily, returning over and over until they were satisfied that the home was clean enough. Children had to join the Hitler Youth. Babies and children up to the age of six were cared for in the children's block in the morning, while their mothers cleaned and cooked. Older children went to school and then spent time in the children's block in the afternoon, learning hygiene and doing physical exercises.

Living in hiding

Jewish people who escaped the **ghetto** or the camps, or who never entered them, living instead in hiding, were called 'submarines'. Life as a submarine was very dangerous.

Papers

Everyone in Hitler's Europe needed identity documents, called 'papers' for short. Anyone could have their papers checked, at any time. Many submarines spent a lot of money on forged papers. Submarines had to be careful all the time. They had to remember the false names and the story they made up about their lives to go with them. They had to be very careful whom they trusted and this was hard for those who were passed along from hiding place to hiding place. Edith Hahn, a Jewish woman who survived the war pretending to remembers:

'...you might never use them, but you had them, you see. It gave you confidence that you were protected and that was half the battle for us submarines hiding among the enemy. If you had confidence the terror and stress of daily life would not show on your face and give you away.'

Edith herself was even luckier. Her papers were actually genuine. They belonged to Christl Beran, a friend who gave Edith her papers. She told the **Nazis** she had lost the papers, and was given copies to replace them. If the Nazis had found out what Christl had done they would have almost certainly hanged her.

The yellow star

All **Jews** had to wear a yellow Star of David on the shoulder of their clothes. Submarines did not do this. The luckiest submarines were blonde haired and blue eyed. Nazi **propaganda** meant that most guards expected Jews to have dark skin, black hair and big noses.

Tivadar Soros was a lawyer. When the Nazis took over, Tivadar was fifty years old, with a wife, Elizabeth, and two sons: George, who was fourteen, and Paul, who was seventeen. This photo of Tividar and the boys was taken in 1933.

The Soros family

Tivadar Soros was a Hungarian Jew who went into hiding with his family in Budapest. They had to survive for over ten months – Budapest was not fully liberated until 13 February 1945. In that short time the Nazis rounded up over half of all the Jewish people living in Hungary, about 200,000 people, and sent them to their deaths.

A big decision

Tidavar heard of the Nazi invasion in March 1944 on the radio. By 1944, there was no mistaking what it would mean for Hungarian Jews. Over the next few days he noticed: 'The first to be caught were people trying to leave: the railway station and roads were heavily guarded.' The Nazis set up a *Judenrat*, a Jewish Council, and put them 'in charge' of all the Jews in the city. Within days the schools were closed. The older children ran errands for the *Judenrat*. One day George was sent to deliver notices telling people to report to a meeting point with a blanket and food for two days. The people on the list were all lawyers with surnames beginning with A–C. 'By the end of the week they had reached the letter G. I decided we all had to disappear.'

Getting papers

Tivadar saw that: 'It was clear we would only survive if we lived as Christians. We needed new identity papers, a new apartment and a new name.' Tivadar tried to get hold of some papers. At first, he got nowhere, but then a friend said he could get birth and marriage certificates (proving you were Aryan) and blank residence forms (to prove you lived in a particular place) with an official stamp.

Yet, Tivadar still needed personal documents – identity cards with photos, labour permits, ration cards, travel permits and military papers. Just as he was beginning to despair, both his brother and the caretaker of a building he ran gave him papers for the owner.

Invaded

The German army moved in to Hungary with their usual speed. This photo shows a heavy tank and German soldiers in a street in Budapest in March 1944, soon after they had invaded.

Splitting up

The Soros family faced a hard decision. Should they stay together? Tivadar decided they had a better chance of at least some of them surviving if they split up. Paul was the first to go. On his 18th birthday he was told to report to a Jewish labour camp. He moved out and began life as a Christian student at the university. George went to live with a Mr Baufluss, who worked for the Nazis but was sympathetic to Jews. Tivadar had most trouble with his mother-in-law: 'She couldn't see the dangers and refused to use a false identity.' Tivadar at last persuaded her to live with a woman who had worked for the family.

Learning a new identity

Elizabeth went to share the home of a friend of theirs. Her papers gave her a German background (less easy to check than a Hungarian one) and made her a Catholic. Tivadar recalled:

> 'I made up all kinds of difficult questions, which she learned to answer pretty well. We did not want her stumbling if the police questioned her. A Catholic friend taught her the **catechism**.'

Tivadar set up a hiding place in a small, windowless room in the building he ran. A Jewish architect friend, Lajos, fixed the room with hidden ventilation, water and electricity.

Moving around

Tivadar was helping others to get papers. He realized he was in danger when people he hardly knew began coming to him for help. Too many people knew about his flat. He moved to a flat some friends were renting:

'The rent was so high that you had to be a war-profiteer or a Jew in hiding to be willing to pay it." He moved from here to the hidden room: "I kept this address a secret, meeting people at a certain church at a set time each day.'

Keeping in touch

Although the Soros family had split up, they met when they could, in public places.

'I met George at the public baths one morning and we exchanged news. The attendant recognized me, but did not know we were Jewish. I met George or Paul there from time to time.'

Tivadar met Elizabeth in a local park and soon found that she was very unhappy where she was and worried that she was being watched. She said:

'There was an air raid last night and I heard one of the boys down there whisper to another: "That's her!" Mrs Zarvics [the woman she was staying with] wants me to move to the country.'

Tivadar said she should go.

A close call

A few days after Elizabeth Soros moved to the country, the Budapest police came to question her, saying she was accused of being a Jewish **communist** who typed and sent out communist pamphlets. She proved she had no typewriter, which threw doubt on the whole accusation, so the police left. Elizabeth feared they would be back and she could not cope with more questions. She fled back to Budapest and Tivadar. They decided she should move to another village. When Elizabeth settled down, George went to live in the same village, pretending to be her godson: 'but I insisted they still lived separately, for safety'.

Eyes everywhere

Paul had been pretending to be a student, but his papers showed he was old enough to join the army. His landlady did not suspect he was Jewish, but kept asking why he hadn't yet joined the army. Tidavar found a way to change Paul's papers, making him seventeen again. This forced him to move on, because his landlady had seen his old papers. Meanwhile, George came back to Budapest, to live with a Catholic family. Tivadar had to move again, too. The Nazis were moving the remaining Jews in Budapest into 'Jewish houses' – Tivadar's hiding place was in one of these.

The Allies invade Europe

The **Allies** invaded Europe in June 1944. These US troops are fighting at St Malo, on the French coast. As troops advanced from both east and west, Tivadar hoped that the Nazis would begin to treat Jews better. Instead, things got worse and Nazi **propaganda** began having an effect:

> 'Crimes against Jews went unpunished. There were cases of people promising to smuggle Jews out of the country then killing them along the way and taking their possessions.'

Too confident?

By the end of the summer in 1944, the Allies seemed to be winning. Soviet troops were advancing from the east, while British and US troops were moving through occupied France. George, Paul, Tivadar and his mother-in-law were all in Budapest. Elizabeth came back from the country, as did many others. Elizabeth suggested it was safe to come out of hiding. Tivadar wanted to wait. On October 15, Admiral Horthy, the Hungarian leader who had worked with the Nazis, said he had made peace with the Allies. Many submarines came out of hiding, but it was too soon. The Nazis simply took power by force and stepped up actions against Jewish people.

The Budapest ghetto

In November 1944 a **ghetto** was set up in Budapest for the remaining Jews. Among the people swept into it was Tivadar's mother-in-law. He smuggled her out, and found her a place to stay with a 'Christian' family that he suspected of being Jewish. Elizabeth quickly went back to the country, while Paul, George and Tivadar stayed in Budapest. Jewish people were herded into the ghetto, killed on the street or deported. People in the Jewish houses were either deported or made to work in labour camps. All this happened despite the fact that the Nazis were clearly losing the war.

Tivadar remembers:

'Conditions in the ghetto got worse and worse. The Nazis would turn up and shoot everyone in a building ... More and more stories leaked out about the German mass extermination camps. Even businessmen who had bought their freedom from Hungarian Nazis were caught.'

The last months

In December 1944 Elizabeth was cut off from the rest of the family by the fighting. Until this point they had been able to send messages from time to time. The Allies were now bombing Budapest and it was dangerous to be out on the street. It got harder for George, Paul and Tivadar to stay in touch. So the boys came to live in Tivadar's flat, pretending to be his godsons. On Christmas Day they opened an unlabelled tin to celebrate: 'To our great surprise it contained pineapple, a treat even before the war. We decided to eat it slowly, spreading it over five days.' Finally, on 13 February 1945, the Nazis were driven out of Budapest by Soviet troops. Elizabeth returned to the city and the family was re-united.

Post-war reunions

This photo shows a reunion of Hungarian Jewish survivors of the Holocaust in Budapest in 1946.

Timeline

1914–18	The First World War is fought. It is ended by the **Treaty of Versailles**.
1923	
8 November	Hitler and the **Nazis** try to take power in Germany by force, but fail. Hitler is sent to prison but is released after nine months.
1933	
30 January	The Nazi Party comes to power in Germany. Adolf Hitler is elected Chancellor.
27 February	Fire breaks out at the Reichstag, the German Parliament
28 February	Hindenburg's decree 'For the Protection of the People and the State', allows for the creation of **concentration camps**. The Nazis persuaded Hindenburg to pass the decree to fight what they called the '**Communist** threat' after the Reichstag fire.
17 March	**SS** set up, formed as Hitler's bodyguard
21 March	Dachau, the first Nazi concentration camp, is set up. Many more follow.
26 April	**Gestapo** (Nazi secret police force) formed
2 May	Trade unions banned in Germany
10 May	First major burning of 'degenerate' books
14 July	Political parties other than the Nazi Party banned in Germany
1934	
7 February	All students have to spend 6 months in the 'labour service'
20 July	SS now in charge of their own affairs – they are no longer part of the army
2 August	Hitler makes himself *Führer*, sole leader of Germany
1935	
15 September	Nuremberg Laws passed against German **Jews**
1936	
August	Olympics held in Berlin
1938	
13 March	Germany takes over Austria, which had once been part of Germany. The Austrian people vote to become part of Germany again.
8 August	Mauthausen concentration camp set up
28 October	First Jews deported from Poland by the Polish government
9 November	*Kristallnacht*: Nazi-led violence against Jewish people: synagogues burned, shops and homes looted
1939	
28 August	Rationing introduced. Covers almost all food and items like clothes and petrol.
1 September	Germany invades Poland. Nazis begin to pass laws against Polish Jews. Soviet Union invades Poland from the east on 17 September.
3 September	Britain and France declare war on Germany
28 September	Germany and the Soviet Union split Poland up between them
30 November	Soviet Union invades Finland

1940

12 February	First German Jews removed from their homes and taken to **ghettos** in Poland
9 April	Germany invades Denmark and Norway
27 April	Heinrich Himmler told to build a camp at Auschwitz
30 April	A large ghetto is set up in the Polish city of Lodz. All Jews from the city and the surrounding area are sent there. More ghettos are planned in other Polish cities for Polish Jews, and then for Jews from other lands controlled by Germany.
10 May	Germany invades Belgium, France, Luxembourg and the Netherlands
15 November	The Warsaw ghetto is set up

1941

6 April	Germany invades Yugoslavia and Greece
22 June	Germany invades the Soviet Union; mass executions of Soviet Jews follow
1 September	All German Jews over the age of six have to wear a yellow Star of David
From September	Mass gassings at Auschwitz begin with Soviet prisoners-of-war and continue. They focus on Jews and become more regular from January 1942.
10 October	The Terezín ghetto is set up; German and Czech Jews sent there.
16 October	Mass deportation of German Jews to Poland begins
28 October	10,000 Jews selected and killed at the Kovno ghetto, Poland
7 December	Japan bombs the US fleet at Pearl Harbor, bringing the USA into the war
8 December	First gassing of Jews, at Chelmno
11 December	Germany and Italy declare war on the USA

1942

20 January	Wannsee Conference outlines the 'Final Solution' to the 'Jewish Problem'
26 March	First major British bombing raid on German cities
30–1 May	Bombing of Cologne

1943

17 March	Bulgaria and Hungary, allies of Germany, refuse to deport Jews
19 April	The Warsaw ghetto revolt begins
11 June	Himmler orders all remaining ghettos to be emptied and their inhabitants killed

1944

23 March	Deportation of Jews from Greece (occupied by the Germans) begins
9 April	Two Jews escape from Auschwitz and send news of the camp to the Allies
15 May	Mass deportation and gassing of Hungarian Jews begins
From June	**Death marches** from camps in the East. Prisoners are marched westward, away from the camps in the east, in front of advancing Soviet troops
6 June	Allied troops land in Normandy

1945

27 January	Soviet troops reach Auschwitz
11 April	US troops reach Buchenwald
15 April	British troops reach Belsen
29 April	US troops reach Dachau
30 April	Hitler commits suicide in Berlin, as the city is occupied by Soviet troops
5 May	US troops reach Mauthausen
7 May	Germany surrenders
20 November	Nuremberg trials of Nazi war criminals begin

Glossary

Allies used to mean the various countries that fought against Nazi Germany, Italy and Japan in the Second World War

anti-Semitic/anti-Semitism prejudiced against Jewish people

Aryan race invented by the Nazis to mean people with northern European ancestors, without any ancestors from so-called inferior races, such as Poles, Slavs or Jews. Aryans were usually thought to be blonde, blue-eyed and sturdy.

asocial Nazis called people 'asocial' if they did not support the Nazi state. Asocials could, for example, be drunks, people who would not work, homosexuals or members of a religious group whose beliefs might make them oppose the Nazis.

blitzkrieg German for 'lightning war', used to describe the German tactic of invading a country at high speed

catechism way of teaching the Christian religion – it is a list of question and answers that summarize the religion

citizen person who belongs to a country and who has rights in that country (such as protection by the law) and duties to that country (such as paying taxes)

collaborate to work with another person or country; in war, to betray your country by doing this

communist person who believes that a country should be governed by the people of that country for the good of everyone in it. Communists believe private property is wrong – from owning a home to running a business. The state should own everything and run everything, giving the people everything they need in return.

concentration camp camp for holding political prisoners – the treatment of prisoners was often brutal, resulting in many deaths

'degenerate' someone who the Nazis saw as having very low moral standards

democracy system of government where people vote for representatives; the people are free to choose who has power and how that power should be used

eugenics a lesson in Nazi schools that taught girls about the characteristics to look out for in a perfect husband and father

First World War war between 1914 and 1918

Gestapo secret police set up by the Nazis in 1933

ghetto area of a town or city, walled or fenced off from the rest of the city, where Jewish people were forced to live

Gypsies travelling people who speak the Romany language; the Nazis used the word 'Gypsy' to describe all travelling or homeless people, or even those whose ancestors had been travellers or homeless

Holocaust in ancient times 'holocaust' meant 'an offering to the gods that was completely burnt away'. By medieval times it meant 'a huge destruction or sacrifice'. It is now mostly used to describe the Nazis' attempt to destroy all the Jewish people in Europe.

Jehovah's Witness member of a religious group that was especially persecuted by the Nazis because they refused to swear an oath of loyalty to Hitler

Jews/Jewish someone who follows the Jewish faith. The Nazis also called people Jews if they had Jewish ancestors, even if they had changed their faith.

Judenfrei 'Jew free' – a place with no Jewish people living there

kindergarten nursery school that children go to until they are six years old

Lebensraum translated it means 'living-space'. Hitler was trying to provide more land for the Germans to live on.

Nazi member of the Nazi Party. Nazi is short for *Nationalsozialistische Deutsche Arbeiterpartei*: the National Socialist German Workers' Party.

'political' person arrested for opposing Nazi ideas or actions

propaganda information and ideas given to people in a way that will make them accept these ideas

protective custody arrest under the law 'For the Protection of the People and the State', passed in February 1933, which allowed the German police to arrest people for as long as they liked without bringing them to trial

race group of people with the same ancestors

racial inferiority/superiority Nazis believed that some races were inferior, that is, not as good as other races. They believed the Jewish people belonged to a separate race, one that was inferior to the German Aryan race (which the Nazis invented). According to the Nazis, the German Aryans were a superior race.

Reich *see* Third Reich

Reichmark (RM) German money under the Nazis

SA short for *Sturmabteilung* – 'Stormtroopers'

SS short for *Schutzstaffel* – security staff. The SS began as Hitler's personal guard. Later, they ran concentration camps and death camps. All the SS swore loyalty to Hitler, not Germany.

Sudetenland part of Czechoslovakia that had once been part of Germany

swastika equal armed cross with each arm bent at a right angle in a clockwise direction. It was the symbol adopted by the Nazi party.

Third Reich means 'Third Empire'. The Nazis saw their rule as the third German empire, with Hitler as the emperor, or *Führer*.

Treaty of Versailles treaty that ended the First World War. It took a lot of land and military power away from Germany.

undesirable word used by the Nazis to mean any person that they did not approve of. People could be undesirable because of their political beliefs, their race, their religion or their behaviour.

Further reading

Auschwitz, Jane Shuter (Heinemann Library, 1999)
Diary of a Young Girl, Anne Frank (Penguin, 1997)
Hitler's War Against the Jews – the Holocaust, David Altschuler (Behrman House, 1978)
I Never Saw Another Butterfly, Hana Volavkova (Schocken Books, 1994)
Never to Forget: the Jews of the Holocaust, Milton Meltzer (HarperCollins, 1977)
Shadow of the Wall, Christa Laird (Beech Tree Books, 1990)
We Remember the Holocaust, David Adler (Henry Holt, 1989)

Sources

The author and publishers gratefully acknowledge the publications from which written sources in the book are drawn. In somes cases the wording or sentence structure has been simplified to make the material suitable for a school readership.

Auschwitz, Robert Jan van Pelt and Deborah Dwork (Yale University Press, 1996) pp. 7, 34
Chronicle of the Lodz Ghetto 1941–44, edited by Lucjan Dobrosszycki (Yale University Press, 1984) pp. 37, 39
In My Hands, Irene Gut Opdyke (Knopf, 1999) pp. 12, 27
Into the Arms of Strangers, Mark Jonathan Harris and Deborah Oppenheimer (Bloomsbury, 2000) p. 17
KL Auschwitz seen by the SS (Auschwitz-Birkenau State Museum, 1997) p. 41
Maskerado, Tivadar Soros, Paul Soros and George Soros (First published in English in 2000 by Canongate Books Ltd, Edinburgh. Copyright © Tivadar Soros, 1965) pp. 45–49
My Heart in a Suitcase, Anne Fox (Vallentine Mitchell, 1996) p. 22
Nazism, 1919–1945, J. Noakes and G. Pridham (University of Exeter Press, 1991) pp. 11, 16, 18
Never Again, Martin Gilbert (Harper Collins, 2000) p. 30
The Boys, Martin Gilbert (Weidenfeld and Nicholson, 1996) pp. 38, 39
The Nazi Officer's Wife, Edith Hahn (Abacus, 1999) p. 44
The Nazis, a Warning from History, Laurence Rees (BBC books, 1997) pp. 19, 24, 26, 40
The Past is Myself, Christabel Bielenberg (Chatto and Windus, 1984) p. 22
Tomi, a Childhood under the Nazis, Tomi Ungerer (Robert Rinehart, 1998) p. 13
War Wives, Colin & Eileen Townsend (Grafton, 1989) pp. 24, 25

Places of interest and websites

Museums and exhibitions

There are lots of museums and exhibitions that you can visit to learn more about the Holocaust and see the evidence first hand.

Imperial War Museum
Lambeth Road, London SE16 6HZ
Tel: 020 7416 5320
Website: *http://www.iwm.org.uk*
The Imperial War Museum in London now has a permanent Holocaust exhibition.

London Jewish Museum
Raymond Burton House, 129–131 Albert Street, London NW1 7NB
Tel: 020 7284 1997
Website: *http://www.jewishmuseum.org.uk*
Or:
The Sternberg Centre, 80 East End Road, London N3 2SY
Tel: 020 8349 1143
The London Jewish Museum regularly features exhibitions and talks about the Holocaust.

Sydney Jewish Museum
146 Darlinghurst Road, Darlinghurst, NSW 2010
Tel: (02) 9360 7999
Website: *www.join.org.au/sydjmus/*
The Sydney Jewish Museum contains a permanent Holocaust exhibition, using survivors of the Holocaust as guides.

Websites

Before consulting any websites you need to know:

1 Almost all Holocaust websites have been designed for adult users. They can contain horrifying and upsetting information and pictures.
2 Some people wish to minimize the Holocaust, or even deny that it happened at all. Some of their websites pretend to be delivering unbiased facts and information. To be sure of getting accurate information it is always better to use an officially recognized site such as the ones listed below.

www.ushmm.org
This is the US Holocaust Memorial Museum site.

www.iwm.org.uk
The Imperial War Museum site. You can access Holocaust material from the main page.

www.holocaust-history.org
This is the Holocaust History Project site.

www.auschwitz.dk
The Holocaust: Crimes, Heroes and Villains site.

http://motlc.wiesenthal.com
The Museum of Tolerance's Multimedia Learning Centre site.

Index

Alsace 10, 12, 13, 15
anti-Semitism 10, 15
'asocials' and 'undesirables' 4,
   7, 21, 26, 35, 42–3
Auschwitz-Birkenau 41

blitzkrieg tactics 6, 13
block wardens 11, 12
bombing raids 24

Catholic Church 30
children
   disabled children 21, 40
   education 16–17
   friendships 22
   Jewish children 17, 22,
      23, 39
   Nazi policies 16–17, 20–1
   youth groups 18–19, 20,
      21, 22, 43
collaboration 9
concentration camps 7, 8, 13,
   14, 15, 21, 26, 31, 38, 43
culture 28–9
Czechoslovakia 5, 35

death camps 8, 9, 35, 38, 39
Denmark 10
disabled people 7, 21, 40

Edelweiss Pirates 19

families
   break-up of 21, 23
   Nazi policies 11, 20–1, 24,
      42–3
   re-education 42–3
First World War 4, 5
food 23, 25, 33, 34, 38, 49
France 4, 7, 10, 12, 14
freedom of movement 31

gas masks 23
gassing 40, 41
'Germanization' policy 13
Germany
   economic problems 6, 26
   foreigners in 25, 31
Gestapo 10, 13
ghettos 8, 23, 32–9, 48–9
Gypsies 7, 35, 41

Hashude 42–3
Hitler, Adolf 4, 5, 6, 8, 14, 16,
   18, 24, 28, 29, 30
Hitler Youth 18, 19, 21, 22,
   43
Hitler Youth Promise 18
Holocaust 4, 5, 8
   public awareness of 9
Hungary 15, 45–9

informants 17, 31

Jewish people 4, 5, 7, 8–9, 13,
   15, 21, 22, 23, 30, 32–9,
   44–9
Judenfrei 8, 15, 17, 32
Judenrat 32, 33, 34, 37, 45

Kristallnacht 30

labour camps 14, 48
Lebensraum 4, 6
leisure and entertainment
   28–9
Lodz Ghetto 36–9

Mein Kampf 8

nature worship 30
Nazi Party 4, 5
   acceptance of Nazi ideas 10
   anti-Jewish policies 8,
      12, 15

family policies 11, 16, 20–1
propaganda 5, 9, 12, 15, 16,
   17, 27, 28, 29, 33, 44, 48
racial theories 7, 9, 17, 41

obedience to the state 11
Occupied Europe 4–5, 10,
   12–15, 27
Olympic Games (1936) 28

'papers' (identity documents)
   14, 44, 45
Poland 4, 5, 7, 10, 12, 21, 27,
   32–3
political prisoners 31
public book burning 28

rationing 23, 25, 33, 38
religions 30
resistance movements 10, 19,
   25

schools 16, 17
Second World War 23, 24,
   48–9
Shakespeare, William 29
Slavs 7, 27
SS 10, 13, 41
state work projects 26
'submarines' 44–9

trade unions 14, 26
Treaty of Versailles 4, 5

unemployment 26

war work 24, 27
women
   Nazi policies 11, 20, 21, 24
   resistance workers 25

yellow Star of David 13, 44